Black Gold, Roughnecks *and* Oil Town Tales

Thanks for your support to the N.F.L. Alumni Association.

Loren L. Kelly

Black Gold, Roughnecks and Oil Town Tales

...as told by a Wildcatter's Grandson

Loren G. Kelly

A Moment in Time Books, LLC

Black Gold, Roughnecks and Oil Town Tales
© Loren G. Kelly, 2019

All rights reserved. This book or any portion thereof may not be reproduced or used in any manner whatsoever without the express written permission of the publisher except for the use of brief quotations in a book review.

To request permission, write the author at:
A Moment in Time Books, LLC
1201 Houston Place
Royse City, Texas 75189

or by email:
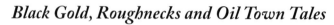
lorenkellyamomentintimebooks@gmail.com

First Printing

ISBN 9781076515827

Book Design:
Vivian Freeman Chaffin, Yellow Rose Typesetting

Printed in the United States of America

DEDICATION

Growing up, I was taught a great respect for family.
Whenever someone asks about my greatest accomplishment in life,
I always respond without hesitation—my family.

It is said our history defines who we are as a people.
The history of our family defines who we are even further.
As a historian and a genealogist, my family heritage is always in my thoughts.

It is for this reason I dedicate this book of prose to my Kelly oil field family.

My Kelly oil field family in 1920.
Seated: Laura Stateler Kelly (my grandma) and Nathan Tompkins Kelly (oil rig driller and my grandpa). Standing (Nate and Laura Kelly's children): Doratha Rebecca Kelly; Luther James Kelly (my father); Hugh David Kelly; Carl Stateler Kelly; Nathan Tompkins Kelly Jr.; and Laura Maitland Kelly (Little Laura).

Contents

Introduction, 1
Wildcat Driller, 9
Oil Field Dad, 11
Hard Hat, 13
Burning Man, 15
On Strike, 17
Company House, 19
Panhandle Dust Storm, 21
Texas Twister, 23
Elephant Rock, 25
Dixon Creek, 27
Oil Town Baseball, 29
Phillips Free Fair, 31
Phillips High School, 33
Mr. George, 35
Blackhawk, 37
Plemons Crossing, 39
Adobe Walls , 41
A Moment in Time, 43
Boom Town, 45
Oilmen, 47
Epilogue, 49
Acknowledgments, 51
About the Author, 52

My dad, Luther James Kelly (far left), his brother Nathan Kelly (second from left), Dad's brother-in-law Francis Painter (far right) and other unknown oilmen taking a break from the oil fields to hunt for food in the Davis Mountains near Pecos, Texas, in 1934 during the height of The Great Depression.

Introduction

In most Texas Panhandle small towns, kids were what we called: "Raised right." We weren't just born, we were "Raised." The turbulent 1960s, for the most part, passed us by. One thing was certain in the small oil town of Phillips, Texas, we all had our heroes. Some were sports figures like Mickey Mantle, Roger Maris, Willie Mays, Yogi Berra, Babe Ruth and Ty Cobb of baseball fame. As a youngster, I loved watching sports and playing baseball on our oil town baseball team in what used to be a cow pasture behind our small neighborhood Quick Stop convenience store in the shadow of the huge Phillips 66 oil refinery. Other heroes were high school teachers, like history teacher Mr. George; coaches, like Coach Chesty Walker; and our well-respected and feared principal, J. Irvin Kimmins (JIK). But my number one hero, as it should be, was my dad, Luther James Kelly. He was an oil field worker, a roustabout, a roughneck and a stillman, who worked in the oil fields and refineries most of his life. His father and grandfather, before him, were wildcatter oil rig drillers, in the late 1800s and early 1900s, 1920s and 1930s. My father had three brothers and two sisters. All of the Kelly boys worked the early oil fields of America with their father, Nathan Tompkins Kelly. It is said there was a Kelly at almost every major oil boom throughout the nineteenth and twentieth centuries. Luther later worked for Phillips Petroleum for over thirty-four years—from the late 1930s to the early 1970s.

    When I was a kid, my dad pointed out constellations in the Texas night sky. On Saturdays he popped popcorn for our family, as we turned on the television to watch Wraslin' and laughed. We both knew it was fake and the wrestlers were merely stunt men. His Christmas gifts were the best, because instead of wrapping them, they were placed in brown grocery sacks. We always knew those packages were special, because they were from Dad. He loved to fish, camp and swim. When I was little, he put me on his back and swam in the lake, my arms wrapped around him and holding on tight. He taught me how to bait a hook, how to fish from the bottom for catfish and use a bobber for bass and perch. He also taught me the art of lure fishing. I didn't know at the time, but as he taught me how to fish, I was learning how to be a man. Dad taught me that my word was my bond and a strong handshake represented who I was. Above all things he taught me family is most important, and I should always remember who I am, where I came from, and our last name meant something and should be honored as he and his father and grandfather before him had done. He would say, "Always provide for your family." These are the important lessons of life learned from my father.

My father was not monetarily wealthy, but was oh so rich in many other ways. With only a fifth grade education he was better at math than I was. He was a hardworking, self-made, quiet man who always worked to support his family, but he was not a social person. We had a special connection as father and son, though he rarely said he loved me. Dad's life was hard, differing greatly from mine. He went to work in the oil fields at ten years of age where he drove trucks, chewed tobacco and smoked cigars alongside grown men. His family traveled like nomads from oil boom to oil boom, living in tents with hardwood floors, cooking outside and doing what it took to survive. Because they worked, the men ate first in his household and women and children ate last—whatever was left over. Once he had his own family, Dad made sure my siblings and I always ate first, allowing us to pick out the choicest piece of chicken, while he ate thighs or wings. He loved reading Zane Grey western novels, Edgar Rice Burrough's *Tarzan* and *John Carter of Mars*. He enjoyed science, specifically astronomy. Dad was intelligent despite a lack of formal education. He was good at fixing things and made wooden toy guns and wooden stools for his kids. I was amazed at how he could build anything from almost nothing, using a saw, hammer, nails, carpenters pencil, level, and measuring tape. He laid cement, repaired car engines, and built fences. He knew how to use a crowbar, a pipe wrench, and a welder. He worked on the plumbing in our house. There wasn't a whole lot that he couldn't do, because in his day you had to have multiple trade skills in order to work and keep a job. He was a carpenter, a plumber, a mechanic, but first and foremost an oilman.

In the early 1950s, when I was about three years old, Dad was working at the Phillips Refinery in Phillips, Texas, when the union went on strike—a strike that continued for several months. Our family ate all we had in the pantry, until we got down to eating navy beans poured over a stale slice of bread before the navy beans and bread ran out. I experienced hunger for the first time at three years of age. Dad was not a union man, nor a company man. He was simply a refinery employee, working to support his family of five, living in a cramped four-room, eight hundred square foot company house.

Dad held out as long as he could to avoid crossing the picket line and being called a scab. But when he saw the look of hunger in his children's eyes, he went back to work. Soon after, three union goons arrived at our house, pounded on our front door, and called him out. Stepping onto our front porch, Luther faced his accusers as they continued to call him out, saying he was a scab for crossing the picket line and they were going to whip his ass. Dad pulled a pipe wrench from the back pocket of his overalls and told them, "You had two months to come to an agreement on a contract with The Company and didn't do it. I waited as long as I could. My family is starving because of you. I'm going to feed my family. I will not let them starve. You can go to Hell! Which one of you wants it first." The union men, cowards all, backed off and fled. They never bothered us again.

In the summer of 1969, after I graduated from high school, Dad and I dug post holes around two acres of land in Fritch, Texas, where we had moved our Phillips House. We used handheld post hole diggers, a five-foot long pointed heavy crow bar to crack rocks, and a shovel. Dad taught me the art of using a shovel to work for you instead of against you. That sixty-two-year-old man worked my eighteen-year-old butt into the ground. I learned a lot that summer. When we finished, Dad told me he did not want me to break my back the rest of my life like he did and an education would keep that from happening. By his example, he taught me the virtue of a work ethic. He did this out of love, because he knew I would have to work to get through life. As a father and a parent, he did what he knew was most important—teaching me how to survive. He once told me, "If you dig ditches, be the best ditch digger there is. Take pride in how good a job you do, because it tells everyone what kind of a man you are. If you make a good hand, the boss will keep you on and you will always have a job and earn a living." He wasn't a perfect man, no father ever is, but he was always there for us. He loved my mother and my mother loved him, until the very moment that he died. I know, because I was there.

In the late 1950s I remember when company men came to our house and told us Dad was involved in an accident at the Plant. Someone had carelessly opened a hot furnace Dad was tending as a stillman in the production of gasoline. Dad pushed the newly hired worker out of the way, saving that man from being burned to death, but in the process my dad was severely burned. I remember seeing my father in the hospital with skin grafts, due to the third degree burns that he had received. As a small boy, I was scared that he would not make it. Many years later, following Dad's funeral in 1972, this same man was one of the oilmen from the Phillips 66 Refinery, who were stringing barbed wire around the two acres of land that my dad and I had dug post holes around and erected posts, three years prior. The refinery workers were there, because they knew how bad my father had wanted to complete the project Dad and I had left unfinished, before he contracted cancer and died. This was an act of kindness by tough oilmen to my mother and our family. Oilmen took care of their own. This man, whom Dad had saved, approached me and told me Dad had saved his life. He wanted me to know he respected Dad and they became friends. My father never told us his burns resulted from saving another man's life. Dad was not just my hero, he was a real hero. This surprising revelation filled me with pride.

When my father found out that he had terminal prostate cancer in 1971, he tried the "chemo" for a while, but finally decided not to continue it because it made him sicker. He had a stroke as a result of the cancer and became bedfast. I watched him waste away a little bit each day from a hard-working man to a human skeleton. He held on as long as he could for Mom and me. Towards the end he was in immense pain and had become comatose. It was a difficult time when he finally "gave up the ghost." I stood by his bed when he momentarily came out of the coma, raised up, reached out to me. Calling me by my name, he asked me to help him. The only thing I could say was, "Dad I wish I could. I love you." He laid back down and returned to a comatose state. I was with Mom at his bedside when he died. Even in the face of death, he taught me how to be a man by showing me how to die with dignity. My dad died at sixty-five—younger than I am now—when I was only twenty-one. He never got to enjoy retirement. He continued working until he died, because we needed the health insurance. I am proud to be his son and he made me the man I am today. He taught me responsibility, love of family, and courage. I think of him often and will never forget him. I love and miss him every day.

Phillips Petroleum Company gave the children of its employees the best teachers oil money could buy. Phillips Petroleum required all of its teachers to have a minimum of a masters degree and some had doctorates, giving Phillips kids an outstanding high school education that prepared us for college as well as life. Phillips was also a "Friday Night Lights" type of Texas town. Football was king in the 1950s and 1960s when I attended the Phillips Independent School District. When game day came around, those students who worked out hardest in practice had the opportunity to play on the mighty Blackhawks football team. Our great coaches paid attention to athletes who displayed both heart and talent. Those students that didn't play football, and the community, overwhelmingly supported the Phillips Blackhawks. This stanza from our high school fight song says it all: "The Orange and Black overall. May they rise to the sky never fall. May we look to thee for our light, and the colors for which we fight." We were "Blackhawk Strong." Our sports teams were legendary for their accomplishments. And because of the academic leadership of our teachers, a large percentage of Phillips graduates became doctors, lawyers, engineers, and other professionals.

We were taught to fight for what we wanted. Our teachers and administrators taught us values, and we could achieve anything, if we were willing to work hard for it.

Phillips High School really cared about every student and discipline was part of the love they showed us. If we got in trouble in school, we received a paddling from the teacher, and then from the principal. By the time we walked home from school, the principal had called our parents. Plus, while our mothers hung the wash to dry on the backyard clothesline, they told the next door neighbor, over the fence, what had happened to their child at school. That neighbor would tell another neighbor, and so on and so on. As a result, every neighbor we encountered chastised us for getting in trouble at school as we walked home. Then, once we arrived home, we usually got paddled again. We could not escape accountability, which made us stronger. We lived in a small town of about three thousand people, where everyone knew what was going on. A place where few secrets were successfully kept.

There is something to be said for growing up in a small town like Phillips. We were insulated from the outside world, which was not necessarily a bad thing. It wasn't always perfect, but nothing ever is. Except for the explosions, poison gas and pollution, we were safe from monsters like the ones stalking America today. Yes, we were disciplined, but with love. Yes, we were micromanaged as kids, but also with love. We were taught morals, respect and values, and had the best teachers. Overall, I believe we had a pretty good childhood. We shared a common sense of pride and community, and we genuinely cared about one another. Phillips was like something you'd see in a Walt Disney movie, and we believed in the fantasy. At least, I did. It wasn't about wealth or winning at any cost, but something you felt in your heart. It was the ground you stood on, the foundation of what you were doing, going to school every day and singing songs like "Working on the Railroad" and "The Star Spangled Banner." We were bound by some ephemeral idea of community—not as a code of conduct but as a wish. We wished to be good, strong Texans and Americans. We wished to practice democracy, and while we had different ideas about what that meant, we were okay with endorsing the American dream.

It's that same American dream that's in danger now, and we all know it. My grandkids are growing up in a different society and country. I am very concerned about them. Respect, by and large, has been diminished in our society. Phillips was a long time ago and I'm saddened this wonderful community no longer exists, but the great memories keep me going. As a former police officer and former teacher, I wish there were more places like Phillips in today's world. Phillips was unique and an exceptional community the likes of which we will probably never see again. Our Blackhawk symbol represented loyalty to our school to our team, to our student body and to the town of Phillips. I believe the Blackhawk Spirit still dwells within those of us who attended Phillips High School. We were and in many ways still are… "Blackhawks."

The demise of Phillips, Texas began when the Whittenburg family, owners of the land where the refinery and town was located, sold the property to Phillips Petroleum. Once the sale was final, Phillips Petroleum Incorporated began encouraging the citizens to move. The beginning of the end was when a major explosion occurred on January 20, 1980. After a long legal battle, Phillips 66 Oil Company evicted all of the remaining residents of Phillips. The entire town was demolished by the company. Phillips, Texas, was effectively wiped off the face of the map by big oil. Access to the area of what was once Phillips, is no longer allowed. A security guard mans the gate to what was Phillips and will not allow former residents to enter. Only the High School Administration building remains as offices for Phillips Petroleum. Phillips is now officially a ghost town and I can never go home.

Phillips, Texas, was a critical part of American oil field history, and its unique culture of blue collar oil workers was like no other. It was my hometown. My father, Luther James Kelly, and my mother, Vivian Madeline Kelly, raised all three of us kids in the oil refinery town of Phillips, Texas. Like his father before him, Luther was a quiet man who worked hard to provide for his family of five. We lived in an eight hundred square foot company house in the shadows of a roaring monster plant, whose smoke stacks belched fire and spewed clouds of pollution and poisonous gas over the roofs of our homes. Luther Kelly labored in this rumble of fiery boilers, greasy engines, pumps and generators for thirty-four years as a stillman in the production of natural gas at the Phillips Petroleum Company Refinery. As a stillman, Luther's job was to transform crude oil into gasoline at the Rice Unit of this refinery. The black gold that roughneck Luther Kelly and his Wildcatter father, Nathan Kelly, had extracted from the ground earlier in the twentieth century was what Luther later converted into gasoline. My Irish-Canadian grandfather, Nathan Tompkins Kelly, was a wildcatter, drilling at every oil boom in America during the late nineteenth and early twentieth centuries. Nate Kelly was one of the best oil rig and artesian water well drillers that ever "made hole." With his four sons working beside him, they drilled for that pitch black liquid gold. I am honored to say my family were oil people and within this unique environment, I was taught how to love, live and survive.

As the storyteller of my family, mine is a story worth telling. For me, family is a sense of pride in who I am and greatly influences how I live my life. My Kelly oil field heritage comprises lasting memories of which I can be proud. Through this book, I have attempted to paint a picture with words that will allow readers to experience a moment in time, a vignette of what my Kelly ancestors endured in the oil fields and how I grew up in the oil town of Phillips, Texas. The Kelly family was a breed of men and women, set apart. It is my hope that my progeny and others will learn from this book, and understand that family history is an important part of who we are as well as who we will ultimately become.

Nathan Tompkins Kelly and my grandma Laura Marie Stateler Kelly, in their heyday. This picture was taken between 1900 and 1910 in Findlay, Ohio. Many of the old wooden oil rigs were constructed by wildcatters during this time period through the 1920s.

My wildcatter grandfather and oil rig builder, Nathan Tompkins Kelly, during construction of a wooden oil derrick in Findlay, Ohio, in 1922. My father, Luther James Kelly, wearing a wide brim hat, is seated high up on a derrick beam with his legs dangling above his father. Other sons Hugh Kelly, Carl Kelly and Nathan Tompkins Kelly Jr. are also posing on the wooden oil rig.

Wildcat Driller

Nathan Tompkins Kelly, burly man, boom days wildcatter
Oil rig driller from the 1890s through the 1920s
Timber derricks hammered together with nails and bolts
Were what this old man and his Kelly boys built

Old man Nate Kelly running the rig and making hole
Roustabout sons tool-dressers, teamsters and pumpers all
Percussion cable tools drilling through sand and dirt into the depths
Chipping away rock to that liquid black gold below

Kelly and sons drilling wildcat wells; hauling casing and tanks of oil
Seeking the world's great gushers on the Kansas, Oklahoma and Texas prairies
A defiant well, taking a kick, toppling the rig, erupting into pillars of flames
Turbulent blow outs shooting high into the oil field skies

Old man Kelly and sons capping an uncontrollable well with dynamite torpedoes
Extinguishing raging flames, ablaze in the night
Killing the flaming gusher that was visible for miles around
Producing an over-abundance of heavy crude

Kelly forefathers driving teams of horses, hauling stacked pipe
Oilers laying and bedding pipelines, crossing canyons and rivers
Digging trenches for pipe with shovels, picks and dynamite
To transport the crude oil, wildcatters mass-produced

Nomad families traveling from boomtown to boomtown
Over muddy winding roads, erecting walled tents on plank board flooring
Transient camp homes miles from town; the fate of oil camp wives and mothers
Men hunting and fishing, women cooking over a campfire; an oil camp rustic life

Oil field pump jacks, nodding donkeys, progeny of an earlier time
Dot the Texas High Plains landscape
An enduring testament and oil field tribute
To my wildcat driller grandpa and his Kelly roughneck sons

March 5, 2019

[left] Luther James Kelly (1971), who worked at the Phillips Petroleum Company, Borger Refinery NGL. [below] Luther James Kelly and his son, Loren Kelly, standing in front of the original Phillips Petroleum Company Alamo Refinery, in Borger, Texas, in the early 1960s.

WILDCAT DRILLER

Nathan Tompkins Kelly, burly man, boom days wildcatter
Oil rig driller from the 1890s through the 1920s
Timber derricks hammered together with nails and bolts
Were what this old man and his Kelly boys built

Old man Nate Kelly running the rig and making hole
Roustabout sons tool-dressers, teamsters and pumpers all
Percussion cable tools drilling through sand and dirt into the depths
Chipping away rock to that liquid black gold below

Kelly and sons drilling wildcat wells; hauling casing and tanks of oil
Seeking the world's great gushers on the Kansas, Oklahoma and Texas prairies
A defiant well, taking a kick, toppling the rig, erupting into pillars of flames
Turbulent blow outs shooting high into the oil field skies

Old man Kelly and sons capping an uncontrollable well with dynamite torpedoes
Extinguishing raging flames, ablaze in the night
Killing the flaming gusher that was visible for miles around
Producing an over-abundance of heavy crude

Kelly forefathers driving teams of horses, hauling stacked pipe
Oilers laying and bedding pipelines, crossing canyons and rivers
Digging trenches for pipe with shovels, picks and dynamite
To transport the crude oil, wildcatters mass-produced

Nomad families traveling from boomtown to boomtown
Over muddy winding roads, erecting walled tents on plank board flooring
Transient camp homes miles from town; the fate of oil camp wives and mothers
Men hunting and fishing, women cooking over a campfire; an oil camp rustic life

Oil field pump jacks, nodding donkeys, progeny of an earlier time
Dot the Texas High Plains landscape
An enduring testament and oil field tribute
To my wildcat driller grandpa and his Kelly roughneck sons

March 5, 2019

[left] *Luther James Kelly (1971), who worked at the Phillips Petroleum Company, Borger Refinery NGL.* [below] *Luther James Kelly and his son, Loren Kelly, standing in front of the original Phillips Petroleum Company Alamo Refinery, in Borger, Texas, in the early 1960s.*

Oil Field Dad

Not a day goes by when I don't feel your presence
I ache at your absence and still miss you
Your shaving brush tucked away in my medicine cabinet
The aroma of Old Spice reminders of you

You were average stature but a strong, quiet man working the oil fields
Labeled oil field trash, a hardened man who didn't suffer fools
Your calloused hands taught me how to use a shovel
Working for me and not against me; an important lesson learned

Wearing dark blue Levi oil field overalls
Your key fob full of jingling keys, hanging down
Your refinery hard hat cocked to the side of your head
Swinging a beat-up black metal lunch pail as you left for work

Not a social man with only a fifth-grade education
But an intelligent man, a skilled tradesman and math whiz
An expert with hammer, saw, level and pipe wrench
You were a carpenter, plumber, welder and cement layer

Gambling with poison and pollution, retiring on your death bed
Showing pride in your work while you lay dying
Teaching me dignity with cancer odds stacked against you
Suffering a little each day as you wrestled your demons

I see you in me, for I am now older than you
Staring at the veins in my old rough hands
Wrestling with my gray hair, scratching my Irish Kelly nose
Realizing, I am now the old man

February 27, 2019

My dad's (Luther J. Kelly) Phillips Refinery hard hat.

A Phillips Petroleum oil field worker, wearing his hard hat, working outside in the blazing Texas sun.

Hard Hat

Oilmen working in oil fields and refineries
Had their custom head gear, using them as skull guards
Roughnecks and refinery laborers, following safety rules
Donning those hardhats as fashionable protective head wear

Refinery control rooms destroyed and oil rig blowouts
With little safety equipment
But keeping a safety hat tightly on top of your head
Seeing you through explosions and debris

How many men did those regal hard hats save?
How many times did a cable or pipe wrench bounce off that safety cover?
In the oil fields of metal rigs and the refineries of machines and boilers
Metal safety hats saved the oilman from concussions and certain death

Hard hats and steel-toed work boots an oilman's best friend
Fancy men in their suits and Florsheim dress shoes and their wives didn't fret
Proud Oilmen wives, hoping their husbands return home after twelve-hour shifts,
Made sure their hard working oilmen wore their hardhats and steel-toed work boots

The hard hat, a savior of the oil worker
Laboring through his graveyard shift
Trying to leave the plant or oil rig in one piece, with all fingers and toes
Not to mention the head on top of his shoulders

Grease and dirt may have smudged that hardhat after a long days work
But when the oilman returned home
He removed his hat, placed it on his grinning son's head
And said a prayer of thanks that he made it home just one more day

March 8, 2019

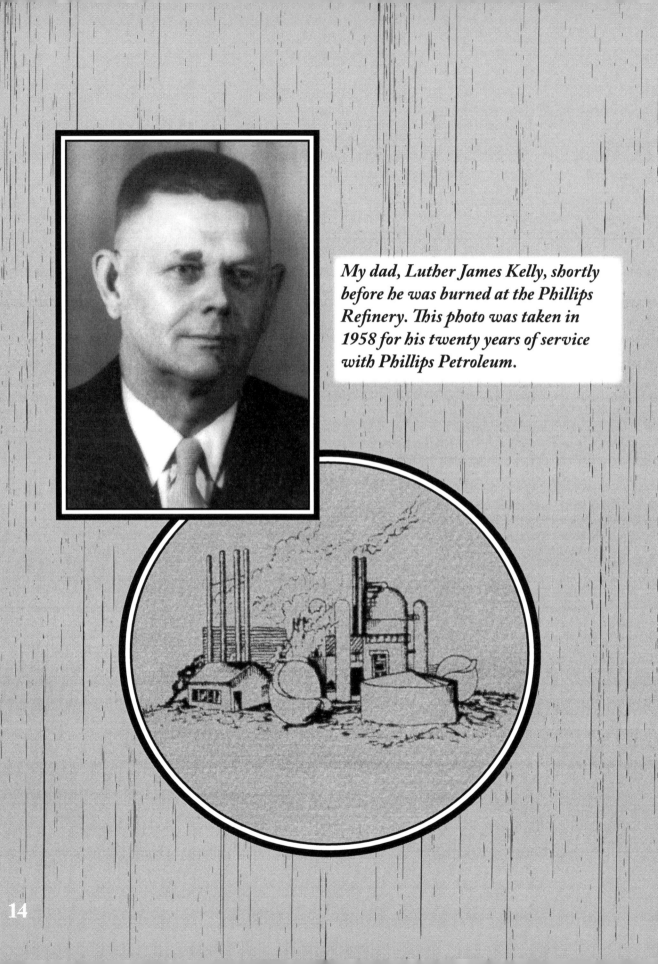

My dad, Luther James Kelly, shortly before he was burned at the Phillips Refinery. This photo was taken in 1958 for his twenty years of service with Phillips Petroleum.

Burning Man
(The Stillman)

A stillman drudging away, providing for his family, refining oil to gasoline
On the graveyard shift at the Rice unit of the Phillips Refinery
New hire cracking furnaces, opening the wrong boiling caldron
Molten oil pouring toward him; the stillman pushes him out of harm's way

But the stillman cannot save himself from that boiling oil
Flaming liquid pouring down his back, transforming him into a burning man,
Flailing arms and legs, he sprints through the plant to escape the unforgiving hell
Wrestled to the floor by oil workers, fire extinguishers dousing the flames

An ambulance's flashing emergency lights and blaring siren
Whisking the brave oil worker away to a distant Amarillo hospital
A roller coaster ride of grotesque pain; a battle between God and Devil
Fading and reappearing, barely clinging to his vanishing spirit

Oilmen with hardhats in hands, wait reverently in the emergency room
Standing like statues in prayer and silence, waiting for the doctor to come
The stillman, struggling for life; doctors tend his charred body as God tends his soul
A little boy holding tight to momma's hand in apprehension and fear

Bloody bandages wrapping third degree burns of this unbending strong man
Enduring months flat on his belly in a rehabilitation burn unit
Grafts from his thighs transplanted to his back, like a scarecrow's patches of skin
Physical therapy of unforgiving torture, battling the unrelenting pain

My father, the stillman, a fighter and little boy's hero
Disfigured, but surviving to work that refinery once more
Never forgetting the sight when he removed his shirt at home
Staring at the scars, not totally healed, left behind by that burning man

March 10, 2019

Loren Kelly at three years of age, during a 1950s Phillips union strike, when he experienced the pangs of hunger.

On Strike

Union oil workers on strike; shutting down the Phillips Refinery
Dad, not a union man nor a strikebreaker, avoiding being labeled a scab
Dodging a beat down, refusing to cross the picket line
But short of money to live and support his family

The strike at the plant, continuing for what seemed like forever
A family surviving on navy beans and stale bread—the only food left
With butter and pepper on top, until all was gone
Our family running out of food, not a scrap remaining

At only three years of age
A small child enduring hunger for the first time
An empty unending pain in a pitiful growling belly
Mom and Dad unable to feed their baby boy

An oilman father peering into his families hungry eyes
A refinery worker finally crossing that picket line
Working hard to earn the money
For his starving family to survive

A union goon squad on the front porch steps
Banging and kicking our front door, almost knocking it down
Yelling and challenging Dad to come out, his family cringing in fear
Dad opening the door, stepping out, calm and cool to face his enemy, unafraid

My brave father, outnumbered, pulling a pipe wrench from refinery overalls
Berating these union scum that he would feed his family and would send them to Hell
Asking which one wanted to go first, swinging that pipe wrench
Cowardly union goons fleeing and disappearing, never to bother us again

March 10, 2019

My sister, Lanora Kelly, standing on the front porch of our company house in 1958.

My Mom, Vivian Kelly, looking out the back door of our company house.

Our company house at 3 Sands Street, Phillips Texas.
A typical house built in the shadow of the Phillips Refinery during the 1940s. Phillips, Texas, a company oil town, was created by the Phillips Petroleum Company fifty miles northeast of Amarillo. The idea was to give refinery workers an inexpensive place to live. In the early days Phillips leased the land and allowed employees' families to have the small white houses with asbestos siding for $4 a room, meaning a four-room house with eight hundred square feet cost $16 a month. The company paid all utilities, painted the houses, sprayed for mosquitoes, repaired the green tar roofs, and fixed the oil-and-gravel roads.

On Strike

Union oil workers on strike; shutting down the Phillips Refinery
Dad, not a union man nor a strikebreaker, avoiding being labeled a scab
Dodging a beat down, refusing to cross the picket line
But short of money to live and support his family

The strike at the plant, continuing for what seemed like forever
A family surviving on navy beans and stale bread—the only food left
With butter and pepper on top, until all was gone
Our family running out of food, not a scrap remaining

At only three years of age
A small child enduring hunger for the first time
An empty unending pain in a pitiful growling belly
Mom and Dad unable to feed their baby boy

An oilman father peering into his families hungry eyes
A refinery worker finally crossing that picket line
Working hard to earn the money
For his starving family to survive

A union goon squad on the front porch steps
Banging and kicking our front door, almost knocking it down
Yelling and challenging Dad to come out, his family cringing in fear
Dad opening the door, stepping out, calm and cool to face his enemy, unafraid

My brave father, outnumbered, pulling a pipe wrench from refinery overalls
Berating these union scum that he would feed his family and would send them to Hell
Asking which one wanted to go first, swinging that pipe wrench
Cowardly union goons fleeing and disappearing, never to bother us again

March 10, 2019

My sister, Lanora Kelly, standing on the front porch of our company house in 1958.

My Mom, Vivian Kelly, looking out the back door of our company house.

Our company house at 3 Sands Street, Phillips Texas.

A typical house built in the shadow of the Phillips Refinery during the 1940s. Phillips, Texas, a company oil town, was created by the Phillips Petroleum Company fifty miles northeast of Amarillo. The idea was to give refinery workers an inexpensive place to live. In the early days Phillips leased the land and allowed employees' families to have the small white houses with asbestos siding for $4 a room, meaning a four-room house with eight hundred square feet cost $16 a month. The company paid all utilities, painted the houses, sprayed for mosquitoes, repaired the green tar roofs, and fixed the oil-and-gravel roads.

Company House

As quick as boom towns began, they started to die
Painted ladies plied their trade at hotels and rooming houses, every man carried a gun
Businesses in town, selling bootleg chalk beer and rot-gut whiskey; homemade hooch from illegal stills
When big oil builds refineries, muddy boom towns transform into civilized company towns

Prefabricated camp housing, constructed in company-owned municipalities
Homes of refinery workers; eight-hundred square foot wooden structures, replace boom town tents
Such were our small white company houses, that all looked alike
We were oil people, toiling through dirty, greasy conditions in oil towns like Phillips, Texas

Refinery explosions shooting fire down our streets
Green chemicals flowing through our neighborhoods
Poison gas from refinery accidents released into our small populace
Families evacuate with washrags over their faces hoping to survive

A mile away women and children wait for the all clear at the Borger Dairy Queen
Not knowing if fathers and husbands were in pieces from explosion or poisoned by gas
Oil dweller's homes, earthly possessions and refinery workers trapped by a police blockade
Returning to company houses at the all-clear, resuming oil industry lives

Mothers and daughters learning how to make do; experiencing hardships and stressful times
Oil town households strong as the oilmen laboring in that refinery of peril
Green roof tar shingles covering their heads; white asbestos siding surrounding four walls
A tiny home of four small rooms where oil families cooked, slept, lived and loved

Phillips Petroleum destroying our houses, evicting residents, turning Phillips into a ghost town
No more churches, no more park, no more schools, no more football stadium, no more company houses
A disappearing act atrocity on an entire community, erasing its existence from the shadows of history
My company home, not a trace left in a town that no longer exists; I can never go home

March 6, 2019

A classic panhandle behemoth dust storm, near Sanford, Texas.

PANHANDLE DUST STORM

Sandstorms of choking dust in the Texas Panhandle
Apocalyptic Monsters of drought and over-plowed farmland
Creations of quick and destructive violent winds
Roll across miles and miles of ranch land

A strong turbulent wind, two miles high
Carries clouds of thick dust into the prairie sky
A dust devil of swirling sand blots out the sun
Turning daylight into darkness

As a child caught in the storm; grains of sand pit my skin
Sift into my eyes, ears and mouth
Covering me in dust and debris
Hard to breathe; a brown affliction of dust pneumonia

A dust bowl tempest envelopes me in a fog of blowing llano dirt
My small frame almost blown away by this black blizzard
Mom removes sand from our house with a shovel
Plagues of grasshoppers and locusts fall from the sky, covering the ground and me

Static electricity builds between the ground and airborne dust
Blue flames leap from barbed wire fences
Playing tag and bumping into friends, unseen in the windstorm
Generates a spark so powerful it knocks us to the ground

The Rain Man causes rain to fall from clouds high above
Turning the dust storm's sand into drops of wet mud
A deluge pelts my body, splatters on my head and skin
Transforming me into a mud-covered zombie

March 7, 2019

A monster tornado threatens the high plains of the Texas Panhandle.

Texas Twister

Rapidly rotating columns of violent swirling air
Stretching from supercell wall clouds to the ground below
Two miles wide; winds moving at three hundred miles per hour
An F-5 monster, the likes of which is rarely seen

Thunderstorms boom in the lower atmosphere, increasing wind speeds to maximum velocity
A monster storm creating an invisible, screaming tube of rising violent air
A behemoth of death, tilting from horizontal winds to vertical funnel, connecting below
A whirlwind of ruination, uprooting trees, flattening houses, dirt flying, ravaging the Texas plains

Before the hellish twister strikes, a frightening calm before the storm
The air thick, stuffy and humid, a lethal still overtakes the atmosphere
The sky becomes a dark green dragon, followed by large hail pelting the ground
Then comes the ear-splitting roar of a freight train

A powerful spiraling demon, its intensity immeasureable
A black angel of destruction, wrecking carnage on prairie communities in its path
Leveling homes into matchstick monstrosities and unrecognizable tangled metal
Tossing cars, cows and people like toys into the Panhandle sky

Aligning the twister with a telephone pole, measuring its direction of travel
Determining which way to run, seeking sanctuary from the murderous ogre's swath
Finding refuge in a storm shelter, a basement, a bathtub, a ditch
To crawl victorious from this herculean beast into a clear blue sky

Tornado alley, a storm chaser's paradise, where killer tornadoes dwell
Storm spotters sighting cyclones and funnels; helping townspeople survive a cataclysmic holocaust
A savage bogeyman psychopath of the skies, strewing debris and destroying lives
Texas twister, a colossal gargantuan leviathan force, earning fearful respect

March 8, 2019

Elephant Rock, in the canyons, close to Phillips, Texas.

Loren Kelly and his dog, Nellie, in his backyard at 3 Sands Street, Phillips, Texas. Together they roamed the canyons near home.

Elephant Rock

There exists a monolithic stone elephant face, near the oil town of Phillips, Texas
Precariously jutting from rough canyon walls, chiseled and weathered by time
Its elephantine body, head and face, a friendly outcropping of jagged rock
For canyon kids to climb; nature's homemade jungle gym

Tributaries of the mighty Canadian cut deep canyons for Phillips kids to explore
Giving birth to the behemoth elephant rock, untouched by the rest of the world
The jumbo pachyderm a monumental testament to our oil town way of life
Flourishing in his canyon home where we played and unearthed our canyon playground

Walking the pipelines, crossing high across the canyons; my dog, Nellie, trailing behind
Arms outstretched, carefully putting one foot in front of the other
Struggling to walk the intimidating pipe, from one side of the canyon to another
Losing my balance, trees intertwined with the pipe break my fall to the creek bed below

Nellie licking my face, then hiking to twin rocks; exploring its rainwater-formed cave
Crawling far back into that claustrophobic dark musty hole deep in the canyon wall
A cool cramped earthen grave for a small boy should the dirt walls collapse
Brushing off spider webs and spiders, as I quickly withdrew from twin rocks cave

Rambling onto the white rock statuesque feature of elephant rock
Staring up at the red rock canyon walls, trying to discern the mastodon's fading face
Focusing to see the colossus mammoth wildly staring back at me
Challenged by this goliath's gaze to climb hand over hand for a better look

Scaling the elephant head, swinging by his rock trunk, climbing further to the top of the canyon wall
Over the top to stand victorious amidst the flint and quartz rocks, sensing a stately presence
Detecting an imposing figure, a paleontologist posing, rock hammer in hand, wearing a dusty fedora hat
Whimsically asking if this was where the fossils could be found, as I stare at him in astonishment

March 18, 2019

Dixon Creek, near Phillips, Texas.

Loren Kelly in 1961, sporting a burr haircut when he camped out on the banks of Dixon Creek, where he gigged for frogs, then skinned and cooked them over a campfire.

DIXON CREEK

Traversing deep sandy loam of early oil strikes, in the center of the Borger oil fields
Rising and flowing from Panhandle, Texas, in Carson County through the Four Sixes Ranch
Running north for twelve miles to its mouth on the Canadian River in southern Hutchinson County
Ending northeast of Phillips and Borger, named for the frontier scout William "Billy" Dixon

As a kid, hiking in the Canyons near Phillips, Texas, with my buddies, along the banks of Dixon Creek
Encountering a wildlife-rich wetland filled with dragonflies, damselflies, frogs and wildflowers
Walking to the river's edge, exploring the shallow sparkling pools of the river breaks
Skinny dipping in the cold clear rain-fresh pools of water

Deep among the marshy reeds and cattails, a young man on a frog gigging mission
Stalking prey with a three-prong trident, burlap bag and flashlight in hand on alert for cottonmouths
Locating croaking frogs with a bright flashlight; shining my trusty torch on their slimy bodies
Bullfrogs dazed by the light's beam, quickly spearing them, flinging them into the burlap bag

Building a campfire on the sandy river bank
Cutting off the frog's legs with a Boy Scout knife; stripping the skin from their legs with pliers
Dipping the skinless legs in egg wash and flour, salted and peppered
Tossing into a cast iron skillet, watching them kick, almost jumping out of the pan, as they fried

Roasting ears of corn buried in the campfire embers; good eating for a bunch of kids
Living large and bellies full, we crawled into our warm sleeping bags
Cozy and dry inside our army surplus pup tents
Falling asleep underneath the star-filled night sky, breathing pristine air

Waking up at dawn to the bobwhite's call and a spectacular panhandle sunrise
Sun rays bounce off shimmering pools of water and dance along the red canyon walls
After a breakfast of bacon and eggs, we picked up our primitive camp, like we were never there
Hiking back to our oil town homes from our Dixon Creek adventure

March 11, 2019

Loren Kelly [first row, far right], about eleven years old, after a hard game of baseball with the Phillips 66 Yankees minor league baseball team for Coach Montgomery, in Phillips, Texas.
[left] A team jersey, advertising sponsors Phillips 66 Cleaners and Hurt's Watch Repair.

Oil Town Baseball

A dirt diamond with a rickety chicken wire backstop on Second Street in the oil town of Phillips, Texas
Playing baseball in an old cow pasture in the shadows of the Phillips Petroleum Refinery
Baseball hat cocked on my head, tapped my bat on home plate, knocked dirt off my cleats
Kids yelling: "Swing, Kelly, swing" as I hit my first home run at ten years old

Grinning coach Montgomery, our Phillips 66 Yankees minor league baseball coach, ready for practice
A canvas duffel full of balls and bats; ordering us to grab a ball and a partner
Tossing hundreds of balls to one another; batting practice with only three swings
Coach hitting fly balls and grounders to the outfield and infield; spinning balls popping out of gloves

At bat, the pitcher throws a fast ball, I bunt, bringing the third base runner home and me to first base
Chewing bazooka bubble gum, blowing bubbles, stuck on first base, waiting anxiously for the pitch
The pitcher tossing the ball back and forth to the second baseman, I try to steal second
Crack of a bat, a high fly to left field, touching second, third, then sliding into home, scoring a run

Chattering at the opposing team; razzing and harassing the batter: "Hey batter! Hey batter! Miss it batter!"
Playing right field, my baseball mitt catching good hits, high fly balls and fast line drives
Trapping the runner between first and second base, tapping him out with my caught ball
The rival team's third out in the final inning; our team experiencing victory, instead of defeat

Sitting in the bleachers, taking a water break, near the dirt road by the oil tanks
Blue jeans with muddy wet knees from slipping and sliding into home plate
Drinking from paper cups, overflowing underneath the team water can
Tired, but happy about the hard game we played, thankful for the win

Returning the following week to our baseball diamond for another great practice
Discovering an oil rig erected smack-dab in the middle of our baseball field
Young baseball players in tears for the demise of their practice field
Only the back stop remaining, along with fond baseball memories

March 19, 2019

Poster advertising the Phillips Fair sponsored each year by the Adobe Walls Lions Club.

Phillips Free Fair

Tilt-a-whirl, scrambler, Ferris wheel and merry-go-round amusement rides
Walking with your honey, holding hands in the multi-colored lights of the Midway
Kewpie dolls, stick canes, boxed popcorn and cotton candy on skinny paper funnels
Carnival barkers calling out games of chance for quarters and dimes to win stuffed bears

Oil town teens helping carnies build the fair rides in the school's gravel parking lot
Assembling fair rides, covered in grease, burning hot from the Texas sun
Sweat and toil paid with tickets for carnival rides or crisp dollar bills
Spending their money as fast as it was earned at the free fair

Working at the Phillips Troop 66 Boy Scout booth
Selling carbonated orange, pineapple and strawberry Fanta drinks
Drinking all the soft drinks we could drink for free
Making hot dogs, hamburgers and corny dogs for the fair goers

The noise of the thrill rides, the smell of fair food and laughter of oil town people having fun
Magical cotton candy machines spinning wisps of a lighter-than-air pink sugar confection
Children with sticky fingers, licking them clean, wiping hands on their jeans
Perfect dome creations of ice in paper cone cups topped with a favorite flavor

The dunking booth with its plank, rigged to fall, dangles over a water tank
Three baseballs for a quarter; thrown at a target releasing the plank
The victim taunting a pitcher: "You couldn't hit a barn door with a can of corn!"
The customer hitting his target, dropping the sitting duck into the cold water with a splash

Arts and crafts exhibiting red, white and blue ribbon winners in the school exhibit halls
Walking in a numbered circle of chairs, sitting down as the music stops to win a homemade cake
Candy apples, popcorn balls, plates of homemade fudge and cookies all sold in the school cafeteria
The Phillips, Texas, free fair; oil town memories of good times, long departed

March 11, 2019

Phillips High School, 1980.

The Phillips High School football stadium announcers box.

[far left] My brother, Richard Kelly, in 1983, standing in front of the Phillips Chesty Walker Football Stadium scoreboard, where he played high school football and [left] wearing his Blackhawk uniform in 1956. A broken leg kept him from completing the season.

Phillips High School

Senior girls in poodle skirts and saddle shoes on Phillips High School "Kids Day"
Boys with duck tail haircuts, hair slicked back, shirt collars-up, a curl on their forehead
High school girls carrying big stuffed Teddy Bears to the school picnic in Phillips park
Tough guys smoking in the park, packs of cigarettes rolled up in white T-shirt sleeves

Avoiding cafeteria lunches, crossing the street to Tisdale's walk-in eatery
Quickly inhaling dough dogs, mustard burgers and french fries, swilling cherry cokes
Shopping at Cut-Rate for bottles of cinnamon soaked toothpicks, hiding them at school
Walking to the Quick Stop, grabbing a Banana Flip, a Cherry Mash and swallowing a Pomac

Rousing Friday pep rallies, the Phillips High School band playing the fight song
Our senior varsity team running into the high school gym as venerated hero athletes
Pretty cheerleaders doing cartwheels in the gym and cheering for the team
Crowds of cheering students in orange and black, rooting for their mighty Blackhawks

Remembering our famous football coach, Chesty Walker; namesake of our football stadium
Coaches teaching respect; making football athletes lift weights, run bleachers, do man-eaters
High school principal disciplinarian, nicknamed JIK, stoically walking school halls
Swinging his well-used paddle, drilled full of holes, autographed by student victims

Signing jokes and remembrances in our student yearbooks on the high school gym risers
Graduating students leaving on their Senior Trip by school bus to Colorado Springs, Colorado
Visiting Garden of the Gods, Cave of the Winds, Pikes Peak and Seven Falls
Touring Canon City Penitentiary and the gas chamber; stark lessons learned

Chalkboards, typewriters and great teachers now gone
The mighty Blackhawk school symbol etched in the administration vestibule floor
Surviving in the shadows of Phillips 66 and in the memories of school alumni
Phillips High School graduates, enduring as Phillips Blackhawks

March 13, 2019

Cecil B. George, my Phillips High School history teacher and mentor in the midst of deep contemplation.

The Phillips High School year book portrait of Mr. George; an outstanding history teacher who acted out history for students, using the classroom as his stage.

Mr. George

There was once a theatrical masters degreed, navy veteran history teacher at Phillips High School
Brought to tears by John Wilkes Booth shooting President Lincoln in the back of the head
Removing his handkerchief from his pocket, wiping his eyes, and blowing his nose loudly
Screaming "Sic semper tyrannis" as Booth had when he leaped from Lincoln's theater box

Acting out the Burr-Hamilton duel; playing both Arron Burr and Alexander Hamilton
Cocking both historical figure's dueling pistols and firing them as Vice-President Burr kills Hamilton
Falling to the floor, portraying the death throes of Alexander Hamilton
Jumping up to stand over Hamilton's body as Burr, yelling: "You defamed me."

Leaving the classroom in a dither, slamming the door behind him, not telling us where he was going
Surprising us by crawling through the classroom window from outside, making his historical point
Saluting classroom students, marching in place, describing General Patton at the Battle of the Bulge
Teaching how Patton read German General Rommel's book; using his tactics against him to win tank battles

Six classroom chalkboards full of notes, students copying feverishly, within the same class period
Talking to himself and slamming books to the floor, as we take tests, trying our nerves
Whistling and shouting baseball quotes: "It's a can of corn" or "Hit big or miss big"
Stressed students attempting to concentrate, answering fill-in-the-blank test questions

Adorned in khaki pants, short sleeve white shirt and straw hat, he left a lasting impression
Dancing as he exits the teachers' lounge, bowing to us as he enters his own classroom
A unique teacher, one-of-a-kind actor of the absurd; bringing history to life on his classroom stage
Teaching life lessons: how to take notes, performing under pressure and think for ourselves

Widely acclaimed history teacher; the best oil money could buy in our small town of Phillips, Texas
Living up to his legendary reputation for many years; entertaining, but demanding
A teaching style creating outstanding students in a history class full of adventure and animated characters
And me, attending university to become a good history teacher; striving to be as great as Mr. George

March 12, 2019

[above] Our Blackhawk symbol, painted inlaid tile on the floor of the old Phillips High School administration building. We were not supposed to step on this tile Blackhawk. [right] A Phillips High School football rally bonfire in the school parking lot.

BLACKHAWK

An old man stands on the rim of a panhandle red rock canyon wall
Overlooking Phillips 66 Refinery and what was Phillips, Texas
Unable to step foot into that ghost town, as dust devils spin through invisible streets
Big oil encroaching on the remnants of what was his vibrant hometown; nothing left

He detects an endangered raptor blackhawk, talons at the ready
Soaring through an orange Texas sky
Searching for prey over its vast territory
Rising to the sky; never to fall

Reminding him of his Phillips High School symbol
Envisioning a huge football rally, surrounding a magical burning bonfire
Blackhawk spirit united with the bright orange flames
Lighting up his oil town's night sky

The orange and black Phillips High School Band
Proudly playing his Phillips High School fight song
To a primitive Indian drum beat; students singing in deep voice harmony
"Go Big Blackhawks." "Go Big Blackhawks."

Students dancing in a circle around that monster bonfire
As the fight song music continues to play
Like Native American dancers of long ago
Reverently sustaining our Blackhawks to fight like warriors

This old man flipping through his Phillips High School yearbook memories
Much older now, than his teenage self dancing around that football bonfire
Saddened by flickering images of what once was
But happy to know once a Blackhawk, always a Blackhawk

March 12, 2019

The haunting one-lane bridge over the Canadian River at Plemons Crossing.

Plemons Crossing

River guide Barney Plemons had an uncanny ability to lead settlers across the Canadian River
Avoiding perils of quicksand bogs that could swallow up a man, a horse or a wagon in minutes
The homestead where Barney settled became a village; Plemons Crossing, an eerie place even in 1893
Known as Plemons, a haunted ghostly place of lost souls, choking on river quicksand

Baby graves filled with infant twins ravaged by the 1918 Spanish flu pandemic
Their final demise in the Plemons' Cemetery, surrounded by rusty tangled barbed wire
It is said you can hear the babies crying, haunting the dark Texas night
Sensing the intense sorrow of their untimely deaths

Ghastly tales told by storytellers around flickering campfires of "Stella's Ghost" and "Stella's Tree"
Where legend says townspeople hung Stella for being a witch
Passersbys of "Stella's Hill," glance fearfully behind them, running away
Her ghostly vision scaring them into the night

Ghoulish "Crazy Jake," roaming the river breaks and ranch land at night
Mumbling to himself and lurking in the moonlight, as he returns to his falling down brick house
Snatching up his shotgun, shooting out his television screen and screaming at folks walking by
His burly overseer tossing another T.V. into the trash heap; grabbing Jake and dragging him back inside

The one-lane deadly Plemons Bridge; haunted by suicidal jumpers and car crash victims
Where scores of people died, running their cars off the side; mangled by twisted metal and broken glass
Murderous bloody rituals carried out on the banks of the Canadian River, underneath
Hangman nooses found, hanging in nearby trees

Old Plemons Crossing, where ghostly apparitions lie in wait,
A sinister black hole in time, lingering memories from those now deceased
Superstitions from earlier days, unspoken evils from horrific nightmares
A legendary ghost town slowly rotting and fading into obscurity

March 11, 2019

Memorials to the frontiersmen *[left]* who fought and to the Indian warriors *[below]* who died in the Second Battle of Adobe Walls.

My mother, Vivian Kelly, and my siblings, Lanora and Richard Kelly, in the 1940s at the Adobe Walls Memorial near our oil town of Phillips, Texas.

Adobe Walls

Hundreds of southwestern Indian braves; nomads following the bison of the Great Plains
Warriors, stretching across the plains, mounted on their finest horses, armed with guns and lances
Noble stoic horsemen, carrying shields of thick buffalo hide against the morning fires of a rising sun
Fighting hordes descending in waves on the buffalo hunting out-post of Adobe Walls by the Canadian River

Galloping like the wind, attacking twenty-eight men and one woman, defenders of Adobe Walls,
A headlong charge of yelling Indian barbarians, bodies splashed in colors of red and vermillion
Bright colors painted on the bodies of running horses, human scalps and feathers dangling from bridles
Multi-colored war-bonnets on half-naked bronze bodies of horsemen of the plains, glittering in the sun

Buffalo hunters firing dead-on, with buffalo rifles, through cracks and holes of adobe house walls
Commanche Chief Quanah Parker, his body painted yellow, immune to the white men's bullets
Besieging the hunters, seeking revenge for slaughtering and decimating the buffalo herds
A moment of destiny bringing redemption deep in Comanche territory of the Texas Panhandle

Billy Dixon raising a giant buffalo rifle, resting it's stock in his sharpshooter's shoulder
Drawing a bead on a mounted Kiowa warrior, statuesque, silhouetted by the rising sun, a mile distant
The loud cannon retort, echoing and bouncing off the blood-red canyon walls, as the bullet whined
Hitting its mark, killing this fierce Indian savage, as he falls off his painted pony into the red dirt below

Bat Masterson witnessing the seven-eighths of a mile shot; heard around campfires ever since
As Billy, a crack shot, took aim with his .50-90 "Big Fifty" Sharps rifle, at the Battle of Adobe Walls
Kiowa and Comanche warriors, two hundred fifty strong, led by Shaman Isa-tai and Chief Quanah Parker
A fight lasting three days; Quanah Parker wounded, discouraged by Dixon's shot; fleeing in fearful retreat

Billy Dixon, the hero of Adobe Walls, making a scratch shot; either the best shot in the west or the luckiest
But this rifle shot that ended the Adobe Walls fight, led to the Red River Indian War; an Indian holocaust
The end of an entire way of life for the Comanche, Kiowa, Southern Cheyenne and Arapaho tribes
Resulting in a proud people's demise; relocation to reservations in Indian territory; gone like the buffalo.

March 14, 2019

This picture is a moment in time of an unidentified man, Amelia Earhart and my paternal aunt Doratha Kelly Painter taken in September of 1928 in Carlsbad, New Mexico. Amelia Earhart was on her way across the country from New York to California and back (to become the first woman to fly round trip across America), when mechanical problems stranded her in Pecos, Texas. Then this chance encounter of Doratha Kelly Painter, adventuresome daughter of wildcatter Nathan Kelly, and Amelia Earhart, a courageous woman pilot. Doratha's son, Robert Painter, donated the original picture to the Artesia, New Mexico, Historical Museum in 1995.

A Moment in Time

Amelia Earhart; first woman pilot to solo cross-country in 1928 from New York to Los Angeles and back
A famed aviatrix flying her Avro Avian Moth Bi-plane; running out of gas in the turquoise New Mexico sky
Strong winds blowing her off course, she spots an open main street in the oil town of Hobbs, New Mexico
Christening the tumbleweed scattered main street of a brand-new boom town, her plane's wheels slam down

Passing the night away in the desolate oil town of Hobbs; a store, a small school, a windmill and jack rabbits
Awakening from a restless sleep, discovering a flattened tire on her bi-plane, nestled among sand and cactus
Amelia, a barnstorming liberated woman pilot, ready for a flight performance, while her tire is being patched
Adorned in aviator helmet and goggles, taking to the air; climbing and soaring into a cloud dotted blue sky

Trying to find her way, high over miles and miles of Texas plains, this flying heroine, becoming disoriented
A map, torn from her blouse and blown away; instinctively following the steel railroad path to Pecos, Texas
Coming down through a hole in the clouds, taxiing to a stop, along the edge of Mexico's Chihuahuan Desert
Amelia airborne again, off into a western sky; her sputtering engine fails: another bumpy emergency landing

This valiant female daredevil aviator descends to a hard touchdown on the dusty Texas desert plains
Hitting a ditch, her plane in a ground loop, nearly turning over, deep in the Trans-Pecos region of West Texas
Her crippled plane towed; dragged amidst thorny Texas mesquite to Pecos, on the banks of the Pecos River
The undercarriage and left wing smashed, the propeller damaged; a diversion from her flight adventure,

Amelia, waiting for engine parts, touring Carlsbad Caverns in New Mexico; visiting with cowboys and oil folk
Oilman Kelly's daughter, Doratha Kelly, another woman ahead of her era; attired in her floppy cloche hat
Inspecting a vast cavern, from Artesia, New Mexico; home of her wildcatter dad, Nate Kelly; drilling for oil
My Aunt Doratha, befriending this courageous pilot; their encounter picture snapped of a moment in time

Amelia Earhart cruising across America, after a trouble-plagued journey through the Southwest
An ominous premonition of her final flight attempt to be the first woman to fly around the world
A lionhearted female aviation pioneer gliding, on the wing; vanishing into the Pacific Ocean skies
Lost at sea, never to land again; her last moment in time

March 14, 2019

My father, Luther James Kelly, and the Harley motorcycle [left] he rode in 1927. [below] He stands next to the 1927 Chevrolet tall boy two-door, steel-wheeled sedan he drove through Borger, Texas, on his way to Artesia, New Mexico. Dad recalled how wild and rough the oil boom town of Borger was at that time.

Borger Jail Memorial – 1929, describing when the Texas Rangers declared martial law and cleaned up Borger, Texas.

Boom Town

Boom towns birthed from oil gushers and prosperity
Laboring oilmen paid thirty-five cents an hour; three to four dollars per day
Pipeliners making five to ten dollars a day; rig builders as high as twenty dollars per day
Lawless revelry and individual hardships soon taking their hard-earned money

Borger in 1927; 50,000 people and three-hundred active oil rigs decorating the Texas plains landscape
Oilmen arrested, filling the jail to capacity, locked within stuffy cramped confines
Prisoners overflowing, chained outside the hot jailhouse, huge log chains attached to large posts
Ankles shackled by smaller lead chains to these log chains, depriving roustabouts of freedom

Slot machines, dance halls and rooming houses; havens of ill repute for ladies of the night
Borger; the "Twenties" Las Vegas of Texas; as many people at night, as there were during the day
The Palisades, Pop Murphy's, and Santa Fe dance halls; ten cents a ticket to dance with a girl
Gambling and slot machines in hotel lobbies; prostitutes standing in lobby windows, enticing customers

Borger's dark Tenth Street active with bootlegging joints and dance halls
Bootleggers hiding illegal stills and moonshine in boom town Borger canyons
Roofed boardwalks on each side of Borger's mile long main street
Parading oilmen drunks on wooden boardwalks, soaked in the rain, mud, blood and beer

Villainous robbers threatening the highways and oil camps
Roughnecks knocked in the head and rolled in a Borger alley way
Thieves hijacking oil field workers; working drilling rigs, during evening and graveyard hours
Murderous shootings and killings; heated arguments between drunken oilmen

Texas Rangers declaring martial law in 1929 Borger as the District Attorney is bushwhacked and killed
National Guard called in by the Governor, enforcing a curfew; Texas Rangers forcing prostitutes out of town
Dance halls closed, slot machines and stills seized; smashed to pieces with axes and sledges
The Law transforming boom town Borger; its wildness and crime cleaned up, as Prohibition came to town

March 17, 2019

Oilman wildcatter Nathan T. Kelly in 1934.

Oilman roustabout, Luther J. Kelly in 1927.

A boom town shanty at oil camp number three in Casper, Wyoming, served as the Kelly home in the early 1930s.

OILMEN

A gusher, spewing oil, blanketing oil workers with that dark liquid gold
Cable tool oilmen covered in the rich wealth of the oilfields
Wildcatter Nate Kelly raising his men's pay with the money he made
An oil field businessman contracting for himself and making more

Laid off, looking for work; no work, no food
Oilmen going where the work was located; traveling from oil boom to oil boom
Some days eating a poor man's meal of Hoover stew like peasants
On good days, eating a chicken and biscuit dinner like kings

Oil rig laborers building shacks in an oil camp on the Wyoming prairie
Kerosene lighted windows shining brightly in the night at the Kelly camp house
Recognized for miles around, a haven for oilmen from a hard working oil field day
Nellie, the oil camp family dog, protecting her territory; home to the Kelly family

My grandpa, Nathan Kelly, oil rig driller, sick and not working his rig, one bitter cold day
With five to six feet of snow, slowing him and his workers to a halt
His four oilmen Kelly son's freezing fingers and toes, unable to make hole
No open winter for oilmen to work in the twenty below frigid arctic Wyoming winter

My Kelly ancestors; roustabouts, becoming hard-working tough roughnecks, with more work time on the rig
A Kelly at every oil boom; toiling as oil pumpers, floor hands, motor hands, tool pushers and drillers
My Dad, Luther Kelly, at ten years of age, driving oil field trucks, filled with pipe and smoking big cigars
Surviving, cramped but cozy in makeshift oil camps; living off the land, fishing and hunting for food

Old man Kelly and sons, struggling oilmen; traveling to Ohio, Kansas, Wyoming, New Mexico and Texas
Oilmen standing in line to work a job; knowing if the drilling boss picked you and you made a good hand
That you got paid at the end of the day, food in your belly and a roof over your head
Incentives for an oilman to support his family; the work ethic that my roughneck father passed on to me

March 18, 2018

My parents, Vivian and Luther James Kelly outside our house in Fritch, Texas—a year before he died of cancer in 1971.

Me and high school buddy Mark Rhoten, making homemade ice cream the old fashioned way on my back porch at 3 Sands Street, Phillips, Texas, in 1969.

Luther James Kelly and Loren Kelly at the Sanford Dam just outside of Fritch, Texas, 1971.

Luther James Kelly putting up fence posts around two acres in Fritch, Texas, 1969. We moved our Company House to Fritch from Phillips, Texas.

Epilogue

As a Native Texan, I am proud to have grown up in the great state of Texas. But in my old age, I sometimes feel like there is something missing. Then I realize that something is my ancestors and my hometown of Phillips, Texas, now a ghost town. A town that once thrived on the high plains of the Texas Panhandle. Nothing left now but dirt after Phillips Petroleum tore down and dug up everything, including the grass. The company literally destroyed Phillips, Texas, as if a bomb exploded and leveled the town. Big oil erased our hometown from history—a tragic end for a great town. If Richard "Racehorse" Harry Haynes had won the legal battle at the courthouse for the Phillips residents, at least we would still have a home to visit. It was David vs. Goliath. Except this time, David was killed when Phillips residents lost their court case and the last holdouts were ultimately evicted from their homes.

Several years ago I traveled to within a few yards of the Phillips refinery where Dad once worked and attempted access to the site of my former home, but a security guard turned me away at the front entrance as if I had never belonged. A feeling of sadness and abandonment washed over me. I couldn't even go to my high school administration building, the only building left standing and now being used as offices by Phillips Petroleum.

Boom towns, wooden oil derricks and wildcat drillers are now gone. Pump jacks dotting the Panhandle prairie, like nodding donkeys, are all that remains of generations of my oil field family. Phillips was one of the last company towns from the historic early boom town years. An oil memorial ought to be erected at the former town site of Phillips, Texas, to commemorate those oil workers. If it wasn't for the townspeople and the refinery workers living next door, Phillips Petroleum would not have been so successful in the oil industry. To this day, it still bothers me that my hometown was demolished, albeit decades ago, but I guess that's the way it is in the oil patch. A mark of shame is often cultivated by castigators who don't understand the oil field culture and label us oil field trash. Personally, I am proud to come from oil people as the son of a roughneck and the grandson of a wildcatter, who got their hands dirty and worked hard drilling for Black Gold throughout Texas and America in the 1920s and 1930s. Oil people take care of their own, which is what I am doing my best to accomplish through this book—to take care of my own by remembering how significant and vibrant their lives were. We were not monetarily wealthy like big oil companies, but we were rich in other ways. Without oilmen covered in grime, grease and pitch black oil, there would be no multi-billion dollar oil companies. Phillips, Texas, was one of many legendary oil towns. The best thing about growing up in Phillips? I have a multitude of happy childhood memories to cherish. The most depressing part is that I can never go home again.

The Phillips Petroleum Company created the town of Phillips six decades ago to refine oil pumped from the Texas Panhandle. The company built houses for its workers, a park and the swimming pool at the school, fixed the streets and gave college scholarships to students.

Now the creator and patron of Phillips, Tex., would be its destroyer.

The company has told the 1,500 residents that remain in the town that it needs the land it owns under their houses and that they have until Aug. 31 to move their homes somewhere else.

Many, although not all, of the residents find that unacceptable. So Thursday night they called in Richard Haynes, the Houston trial lawyer better known as Racehorse Haynes in these parts, a man regarded here as a legal magician. "Corporate Phillips" vs. Texans

"I ain't here for no money," he told about 400 blue-collar residents gathered in the high school auditorium. Nor was he seeking fame, he said, since "I've already been famous."

The issue, Mr. Haynes said, was whether "corporate Phillips" can "push Texas Americans around" without a fight. "This is not a third-world country," he added. "This is the Panhandle of Texas."

—"Oil Company Town, Facing Eviction, Digs in for Legal Battle"
Robert Reinhold, Special to *The New York Times*
February 23, 1986

ACKNOWLEDGEMENTS

First and foremost, praise and thanks to my Lord Jesus Christ, who has been with me every step of the way throughout my life.

Many thanks and much gratitude to my hometown of Phillips Texas, now a ghost town, and all of its former residents, for giving me a true sense of my life's purpose. The community of Phillips will continue to thrive in the memories of all Phillips Blackhawks.

Sincere thanks to Herldine Radley, M.L.S, head librarian of the C. F. Goodwin Public Library in Royse City, Texas, for telling me… "Sure you can write a book." She was instrumental in assisting me to ignite my passion for writing this book.

I cannot express enough thanks to author Millie Jean Coppedge for her positive affirmations and guidance. She inspired me, through her professional advice, that I was a good writer and encouraged me to get this book published. Her advocacy was invaluable.

A special thank you to my editor, Vivian Freeman Chaffin of Yellow Rose Typesetting for her fantastic job of editing. It was a rewarding experience to see my dream of writing a book come to life. The final manuscript is exactly what I wanted to accomplish—combining my creative poetry with genealogy and history to tell the story of my oil field family. Writing this book was almost like birthing a baby. I describe an editor as being like a midwife or a doctor helping to birth the writer's work. William Faulkner once gave a piece of advice to aspiring young writers that you have to learn, to "kill your darlings." In other words, you have to get rid of your most precious and especially self-indulgent passages for the greater good of your literary work. Ms. Chaffin helped me achieve this feat. Experiencing the editing process with her has made me a better writer.

Most important, a loving thanks to my family and to my beautiful wife and soulmate, Barbara Kelly, whose patience and enduring support during this process kept me going. Barbara, I promise not to stay up late at night writing. Well… at least for now I will take a break. And of course I ardently thank my Kelly ancestors (including my parents and grandparents), who exemplify the very soul of *Black Gold, Roughnecks and Oil Town Tales*. Ultimately, this book is a lasting legacy I can pass down to future generations of my family and share with readers, which was my original intent.

About the Author

Loren G. Kelly graduated from Phillips High School, Phillips, Texas, in 1969. He subsequently attended Frank Phillips College, Borger, Texas, and earned an Associate of Arts degree with honors, as a member of Phi Theta Kappa (The International Junior College Honor Society) in 1971. Loren continued his education at West Texas State University, Canyon, Texas, graduating with a Bachelor of Science in History and a Secondary Social Studies Teacher's Certificate in 1974. He was also a member of Phi Alpha Theta (The International Honor Society of History), while at West Texas State University (now West Texas A&M University).

Loren retired from Dallas County following twenty-six years of service and a total of thirty-nine years in criminal justice (1977-2016). Loren is a 1987 graduate of the Dallas County Sheriff's Department Police Academy. He married his beautiful wife, Barbara, in 1981 and they have four children, Shaun, Michael, James and Rachel, as well as eleven grandchildren. He and Barbara love to travel, having visited Ireland, England, France, Switzerland, Italy, Canada and Hawaii since retiring. Loren is a Christian and active member of Community Baptist Church in Royse City, Texas. He is a member of the Royse City Cultural Arts Committee that oversees the C. F. Goodwin Public Library and the Zaner Robison Historical Museum. A writer and avid reader/researcher of history, Loren is also a genealogist who enjoys researching family history.

The Author, Loren G. Kelly, with his wife, Barbara, 1998.

Made in the USA
Columbia, SC
21 July 2019